# Living with Norwegians

## The guide for moving to and surviving Norway

Sean Percival

# Table of contents

# Who this book is for

**Expats**

Non-Norwegians moving to and living in Norway

**Love refugees**

Recently moved to Norway for love? You're going to need a guide (and a lot of wool!)

**Norwegians**

Norwegians looking to better understand the challenges foreigners face when moving to Norway

**Corporations**

As a welcome guide to new international staff working in Norway

**Gifts**

The ultimate gift for anyone curious about or moving to Norway

# About this book

This guide is a collection of personal experiences, Norwegian stereotypes, and friendly advice on how to survive life in Norway. It's the ideal starting point for someone who is curious about life in Norway and for those already in the process of making the move. Learn how to adapt to life in Norway and better understand the sometimes-peculiar Norwegians themselves.

After reading this book you'll be better prepared for the challenges Norway will throw at you. And you, regardless of your country of origin or status, will be challenged by life in Norway. However, through these challenges you might just come to love Norway. Although it's not an easy country to love sometimes, you have to work hard for it. You have to struggle sometimes to be worthy of the great honor of having Norway love you back. This struggle before the reward is actually the Norwegian way.

The book is organized into several sections. It's not meant to be some concrete "dos and don'ts" guide or heavy academic work on the intricacies of Norwegian society. Although it will tell you over 50 things you can try to not only survive Norway but hopefully thrive as well.

Be sure to visit **livingwithnorwegians.com** for even more Norway survival tips and updates. Some links found on the website and in this book may contain affiliate codes; by purchasing these products you're helping to support this book. I appreciate that, and you will too once you realize how damn expensive everything is in Norway.

For more help better understanding Norwegian work culture be sure to check out the companion book to this one, *Working with Norwegians* (ISBN **9798629630937**). The book is available in all Norwegian book stores, direct at **percivalpublishing.com**, or from online retailers such as Amazon.

Look for these QR codes throughout this book. Scan them with your phone's camera to get an instant link to the resources mentioned on that page. Give it a try now to visit the official website for this book.

# About the author

Sean Percival is an American investor, author, and entrepreneur originally from California. He has lived in Norway for more than five years now, which by his account means he knows what the hell is going on at least half the time in this country. The other half he's just as confused as the many other foreigners in Norway. That's why he wrote this guide for you.

Growing up in large metropolises Los Angeles and San Francisco, Sean was in for quite the culture shock when he moved to Norway. Despite his personal experience both in business and with many diverse cultures, he struggled like so many other foreigners do when they make the move to Norway. However, through this experience he learned that he was not alone. In true "pay it forward" style, he has become somewhat of an authority on helping expats get their bearings in Norway and better understand the Scandinavian culture.

During his time in Norway, Sean has lived in Oslo but now spends most of his time in the summer village of Larkollen. From here he helps support Norwegian entrepreneurs through his work with Innovation Norway and other ventures. He also runs a small publishing company not-so-modestly called Percival Publishing.

# WELCOME TO NORWAY!

"Welcome to Norway!"

This is a phrase I often heard after arriving in Norway. At first, I didn't quite understand the saying, perhaps taking it too literally.

"Yes, I'm here, and thanks, I do feel welcome," I would think to myself.

Over time I would come to understand that these three simple words best captured the Norwegian experience for a foreigner like myself. For us, things are just a little different here.

"Let's go jump in that freezing cold fjord!"

—Welcome to Norway!

"It's Friday so we must make tacos! With cold corn!"

—Welcome to Norway!

"A popular Norwegian TV station once broadcast an entire eight-hour train ride. It was watched by millions of Norwegians."

—Welcome to Norway!

Yes, Norwegians are unique, proud, and incredibly special. The country has a rich history that includes many periods of hard times well before the good times the modern Norwegian enjoys today. This history has shaped the way Norwegian society operates. If you were to look at just about any world report on the status of the various countries, it would appear that despite some peculiar ways of doing things, everything is working very well in Norway.

One could go on and on about all the positives of life in Norway. But this book isn't an attempt to try to sell you on the country. Chances are if you're reading this you're already here or you're about to make the move. In either case, you're in the right place.

This book is instead a collection of tactical tips and observations I've made over the years living in Norway and with Norwegians. My hope is that they can help us better understand each other and perhaps make it a bit easier to get used to life in this unique country.

# WHAT TO PREPARE AND PLAN

Before I get started, let's get through some of the more boring and practical things. If you're already living in Norway, you can probably skip ahead. For everyone else new to Norway, it's important to know that Norwegians love to plan. They create a plan for the plan and backup plans for both plans. I've personally sat in meetings for work where the whole purpose was to plan a future meeting. When it comes to preparation and planning, Norwegians love it almost as much as cross-country skiing.

Personally, I don't mind planning, but at the same time my favorite quote is

*"Everyone has a plan, until they get punched in the face."*

- Mike Tyson

However, this is not how the Norwegians work. It's all about reducing risk, even if that means lots of planning before you do anything. You also need to make sure there's strong consensus in every part of life. Everyone must be on board and must have reviewed the plan, agreed to the plan, not agreed on a small detail, agreed again on the plan, and then finally, set up a planning meeting to get started.

So do as the Norwegians do, and let's start preparing and planning for life in Norway.

# Test Norway a few times

WHAT TO PREPARE AND PLAN

You've been reading all the articles about the high quality of life in Norway. You've been browsing Instagram looking at all the wonderful Norwegian nature porn of the northern lights. Perhaps you know someone who knows someone who won't stop raving about their great life in Norway. And like many who move to Norway, you're probably also looking for a fresh start or at least an upgrade to your current life. However, before you jump headfirst into the fjord there's something you should know.

Moving to and surviving Norway is not easy. In fact, it's quite difficult.

All that shimmers on those Instagram posts is not gold as it turns out. While moving and adjusting to any new country can be tough, Norway is especially challenging. This is evident in the way Norwegians inquire when they first meet you by asking directly, "Welcome to Norway! Do you plan to stay?" That comes off as especially rude to a new arrival. So much for feeling welcome, right? They ask this because they have seen many foreigners before you try to live in Norway and fail. Truth be told, many do not even last their first year.

You'll learn more in this book about how to survive life in Norway, but before you do make that leap you absolutely should do a few test visits just to be sure. There are many little challenges that add up when it comes to adjusting to life here. Best to be both prepared and certain that you're ready for such a change. It's also recommended that you do one of these trial visits during wintertime. Because if you can make it through even a single brutal Norwegian winter, you're probably already half the way to surviving Norway.

To get a good overall picture of life in Norway, I recommend visiting not just Oslo the capital city but a few other major cities such as Bergen and Trondheim. Along the way to those cities you'll also get a chance to experience some of the many smaller villages of Norway. And of course, treat yourself to some of that delicious Norwegian nature porn you've seen so much of.

# Join an expat Facebook group

WHAT TO PREPARE AND PLAN

As the saying goes, “misery loves company,” and you won’t find any better company than your fellow countrymen and women. Not only do they speak your language (literally), they can really help you as you adjust to life in Norway. And the best place to find them even before you make the move is on Facebook, specifically within Facebook groups. There is an “expats in Norway” Facebook group for just about every country of origin, and they tend to be very active, not to mention full of people who are willing to help a new arrival. They, of course, were in your shoes at some point and understand some of the challenges of moving to Norway.

To find them, simply open Facebook on the web or mobile app and search away. Using some variation on the below search terms will help you find your tribe. Join the group and don’t be shy. However, before you ask a question to the group it’s recommended to search the group for previous posts that might cover your own question. Thanks to this book, you should also already know most of the basics.

“Americans living in Norway”
“British Expats in Norways”
“Expats in Oslo”

**Expat Facebook Group**

**bit.ly/NorwayExpats**

# Finding a job in Norway

WHAT TO PREPARE AND PLAN

Entire books can and have been written about how to find a job in Norway. Ideally, you already have a job lined up before making the move to Norway. Truth be told, as a foreigner (especially from a non-EU country), having a job will typically be required before you can even consider relocation. If you're immigrating from an EU country, you have a bit more leeway in getting started in Norway because you can stay for six months while finding employment.

For everyone else, it's actually an uphill battle finding a job in Norway. In a small country, there are not that many open jobs available overall. At the same time, Norwegians tend to hire other Norwegians over foreigners. This is partly due to the language barrier, even though most Norwegians speak English very well.

But it really comes down to the fact that Norwegians simply trust other Norwegians more than other nationalities. It's not to say Norwegians aren't inclusive, because they are. It's just that in Norway trust is everything, and this can only be built over many years. As a newcomer, you are essentially starting at a negative trust level, so your first job will be difficult to obtain. Each job role after that will be progressively easier to find.

Finding a job is a complex topic and heavily dependent on what type of work you're ultimately looking for. So I can only give you three pieces of advice to get you started:

- Finn.no is the largest job site in the country and worth browsing to get a better understanding of what types of jobs are available. For foreigners, jobs in the area of IT are typically the easiest to find a match with and don't come with much Norwegian language requirement.

- It's recommended to also locate Norwegian companies of interest and check their websites to get the most up-to-date job postings.

- Finally, and perhaps most importantly, referrals are how many Norwegians find new jobs. If you can get a referral from a friend or previous colleague into a Norwegian organization, you're much more likely to make it to the interview stage.

Good luck!

You're going to need it.

# Navigating UDI

WHAT TO PREPARE AND PLAN

As you prepare to get settled in Norway, you'll no doubt be spending some time with UDI, which stands for the inappropriately long *Utlendingsdirektoratet*, aka the Norwegian Directorate of Immigration. It holds all the keys to immigration, work or resident permits, and Norwegian citizenship.

Some fellow expats might be prone to complaining about the bureaucratic and long process of dealing with UDI, although my experiences have been mostly positive. Compared to, say, the government bodies of the United States, UDI is remarkably transparent and uses very modern digital systems. That being said, it's still a big, slow-moving government organization, and you're likely to encounter some snags as you weave your way through such a system. Additionally, thanks to Norway's rise as a desirable place to live for both expats and refugees, at times UDI can become overloaded.

Your best bet is to read through its entire website for the articles that pertain to your situation. They are rather clear and easy to understand, and the majority of them are available in English and several other languages. When in doubt or unsure of what step to take next, drop a question to your fellow expats in the Facebook groups mentioned previously.

There is only one important thing to know when dealing with UDI, and that is it does not make exceptions. The requirements to obtain residency are spelled out quite clearly in its materials. You either check all the boxes and get approved or you do not. In a country with extreme equalitarian views, no one skips the line or steps ahead in the process. Regardless of who you are, where you came from, or the wealth you have, everyone is treated equally in Norway.

**UDI Website**

**udi.no**

# Getting your D-number

WHAT TO PREPARE AND PLAN

Should you manage to successfully navigate UDI and obtain your resident permit, you'll next be issued a D number. This is a temporary identification number given to expats. Norwegians citizens themselves use a national ID number for the same purposes as a D number.

Much like a Social Security number in the United States, the D number is your unique identification code. It's used in many aspects of life in Norway such as obtaining a bank account, renting an apartment, and so on. It's also used as part of your tax records.

Depending on your situation you might be issued either a D number (typically for stays of less than six months) or a national ID number (if you're planning to stay longer).

Your D number consists of your birthday (written DD-MM-YY) followed by a code. This is a number you can freely give out when asked for and not something you need to protect or hide. Norway is a country of great transparency, so such information is shared freely.

# Finding housing in Norway

WHAT TO PREPARE AND PLAN

Most foreigners who relocate to Norway typically rent before purchasing a property. This allows you to better understand the region you're moving to before having to dive into the very competitive real estate market. Therein lies the problem: Norway is a "buyer's market" with the majority of native Norwegians owning property. In fact, many Norwegians own several properties, and it's not uncommon for even young Norwegian adults to own an apartment.

That can actually be helpful for renters because it makes the rental market much less competitive for them. That being said, there is not a huge amount of inventory available, and in markets such as Oslo the best places do go quickly.

To get you started here are three good options for finding housing:

- Finn.no is Norway's largest classified website has perhaps the largest amounts of rental available. Setup alerts to get notified when new rentals come on the market.

- Hybel.no is another housing website that focuses primarily on the renter market with all content available in English. This is mainly for student housing.

- Friends and coworkers: Another great option for finding a place is to simply ask your Norwegian friends and colleagues. Often, they know of rentals that are yet to be posted. As a bonus you might be a familiar neighbor, although thanks to Norwegians' general shyness you'll probably never actually have to talk to them.

There are many other considerations when renting in Norway, but it's worth noting the biggest shock to new arrivals is often the large deposit required to rent a place. Typically, this amounts to three months' rent and must be paid before you move in. The deposit is held in an escrow account and returned to you after you vacate the apartment. This is in addition to paying the first month's rent as well.

If you're on a smaller budget, a college student, or just want to be more social, then you might want to consider moving into a collective (known as *kollektiv* or *bokollektiv*). This is where a few residents come together to rent one large place. Typically, everyone gets their own bedroom but areas like the kitchen are shared spaces.

# Forwarding your phone number

WHAT TO PREPARE AND PLAN

After arriving in Norway, you'll quickly find out that you'll need a new local mobile number with a Norwegian provider, not only for ease of receiving phone calls but also to access various financial and government systems using BankID. So, the question will quickly come up: What to do with your old number?

It's likely and recommended to retain access to your old number so contacts can keep in touch and you can continue using it for internet services that require it for authentication, (aka 2FA or two-factor authentication). If you disable your old phone number, you may find it's difficult to log in to some of your favorite online services.

The simplest solution for continuing to receive both text messages and voicemails is to use Google Voice. This service, offered free by Google, is what might be called a virtual phone number. It allows you to access these messages from anywhere with an internet connection, regardless of who provides your mobile phone connection. It's all done with the Google Voice app.

**Google Voice**

**bit.ly/NorwayGoogleVoice**

# Keeping a post box back home

WHAT TO PREPARE AND PLAN

Even when moving countries, it's hard to break all ties. There might, for example, be reasons you still need to receive mail back in your home country. This can be especially important for receiving notifications from the government and for other purposes such as for credit card statements.

In most cases you will not be able to forward your physical mail to Norway. On a related note, you'll be happy to hear that you don't receive much physical mail in Norway thanks to a strong digitization of government-related and other important paperwork.

When it comes to mail from your country of origin, you have two options. The first is to use a family or friend's address and set up a mail forwarder to there. This works especially well with your parents.

The next option is to set up a VMS (virtual mailbox service). The way they work is they provide you with an address, similar to a PO Box, and receive your mail for you. They then scan the mail for you and allow you to access it directly from a web browser or phone.

For my fellow American expats, I recommend using Earth Class Mail for your VMS service.

**Earth Class Mail**

**bit.ly/NorwayMail**

# Stock up on meds and vitamins

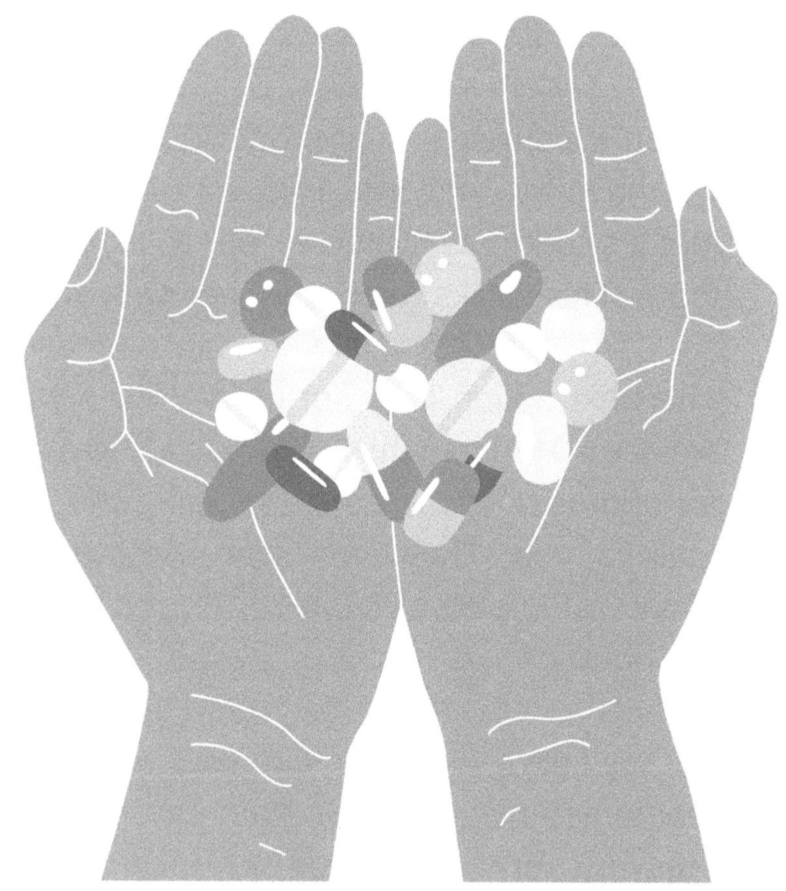

WHAT TO PREPARE AND PLAN

Every country is different when it comes to the types of over-the-counter medicine one can buy. In the case of Norway, you'll find that this is not a culture that does much self-medication, at least with regard to typical nonprescription medicines found around the world. I suppose for Norwegians the excessive drinking is self-medication enough!

As a foreigner in Norway, however, that might leave you without access to your favorite drug store cold medicines and even the most basic vitamins. The truth is, there is very little of either available in Norway, or what is available can best be described as very, very wimpy. Usually, the local Norwegian versions have low dosage amounts, and your options are also extremely limited.

If you need to chug an entire bottle of Nyquil to get to sleep at night, I'm not one to judge, but to a Norwegian this would seem very strange, perhaps borderline drug abuse. If you speak to any Norwegian about not feeling well, even if that person is a doctor, they'll probably recommend a few simple remedies. These usually consists of taking a mild painkiller (known locally as *paracet*) or having some fish oil (yuck!), and they will also recommend you go take a walk to get some fresh air and sun. Yes, for Norwegians the cure to whatever ails you is almost always nature.

However, if those aren't going to cut it, or you have very specific needs, you have little choice but to join the underground drug smuggling ring of us fellow expats. This takes the form of cramming your suitcases with medicines each time you return from your home country. It is not recommended to try to have these medicines mailed into Norway because they can often be discovered by the customs department and confiscated.

A few more pro tips: most of the medicines from outside of Norway are not allowed in the country, but if you're traveling into Norway, you're allowed to bring anything needed for the duration of your visit. To avoid raising too much suspicion, don't bring an excessive amount of any single medicine. It also helps to open the packaging and make it appear the product is actually being used. If you, for example, roll up with twenty boxes of unopened aspirin, it'll be difficult to argue you need so much for your time in Norway.

**iHerb Online Store**

**bit.ly/NorwayiHerb**

You can also find some health needs from online retailers such as iHerb. Just note that because these retailers are typically outside of Norway, you may need to pay a custom tax to import products.

# Transferring money across borders

WHAT TO PREPARE AND PLAN

To get established in Norway and to maintain your obligations back in your home country, you'll likely need to transfer money across borders. For many expats like myself this is a task that we need to do several times a month.

The banking system in Norway is incredibly well structured with inexpensive (basically free) options for transferring money domestically. When it comes to international money transfers, it can sometimes be more difficult, especially when transferring money to and from countries outside the EU. This was certainly the case for me coming from the United States, a country that, despite its wealth, has very archaic and in many cases expensive options for international wire transfers.

Thankfully, much like how Uber made it easier for us to get around and Tinder made it easier for us to get laid, there's a new app for that. It's called Wise.com This online service makes it incredibly easy and cost-effective to move money around the world however you please.

It charges modest fees and gives you very fair currency conversion prices as well. On top of this, Wise.com offers additional services such as bank accounts, debit cards, and business services.

# Netflix and chill with a good VPN

WHAT TO PREPARE AND PLAN

In order to access certain shows on services such as Netflix and, in some cases, access certain websites back in your home country, you'll need a VPN. That stands for virtual private network, and essentially it allows you to hide your current location while also spoofing your location. You are in some sense teleporting your internet connection to a different part of the world and routing your own traffic through that location. This also provides additional privacy to your online use because your internet provider can no longer see what websites you visit or services you use.

VPNs can be especially useful in Norway because many streaming services have a very limited catalog here. And as you might expect, much of the content is from the local market and in Norwegian. So, what happens if you want to binge watch all your favorite episodes of "Friends," for example? That's where the VPN comes in handy and allows you to "trick" Netflix into thinking you're actually in the USA or another location with broadcast rights to the content you want to watch.

There are many providers of VPN services, but in my experience the best is NordVPN. It offers fast and reliable access at a great price. Scan the below QR code to get a special signup discount.

# GETTING SETUP

If you have been to Norway already then you already know. There's something special about just landing in the country. There's a calmness in the air together with the sometimes brutally cold weather. There's a different motion, a different flow to the country and the people that occupy it. And, like well-designed Scandinavian furniture, it's intoxicating to look at.

I'm happy to share that the nice feeling of arriving in Norway doesn't change even after many years and many return visits. Regardless of where you go in the world, it always feels good to come "home" to Norway. It always feels safe.

For the new arrivals, here's a few things you'll want to do to get started on living with Norwegians and your new life in Norway.

# Getting to know the glory of duty free

GETTING SETUP

As you'll quickly learn, in Norway things are damn expensive. On top of that, the tax is high on pretty much all goods. And while many Norwegians will tell you they enjoy paying taxes because they get so many good social services as a result, there's one place where they truly enjoy skipping out on taxes. That place is the duty-free store.

Found at major airports such as Gardermoen in Oslo, the duty-free store sells just about everything you can imagine, from beauty care products, to candy, and of course, tobacco and alcohol. The last two are especially popular goods to purchase because you'll save a significant amount, in some cases almost half of what you would typically pay within Norway.

So this is your chance to stock up, and stock up is what Norwegians do at duty-free. It's almost a comical scene to see them with arms full of their beloved treats. Jet lag be damned, everyone who wants to get a good deal makes time to shop duty-free before they pick up their luggage.

# Setting up a local Norwegian cell phone

GETTING SETUP

Norway is a highly digitized society. A cell phone isn't just important for staying in touch; it's a critical tool for navigating the country and using various services. Your cell phone from your home country is likely to still work in Norway. However, you also risk running up a large bill or having limited access to mobile data. So you'll want to get your SIM card swapped out with a local Norwegian provider soon.

If you've already established your residency and have a D number, then you can start a new cell phone plan with any of the major providers. If you're still in the process of getting your D number, then you'll only be able to purchase a prepaid plan.

The two major cell phone providers in Norway are Telenor and Telia, although there are several smaller and, in many cases, cheaper options as well.

Depending on where you come from, you may notice your mobile data is fast, like blazing fast. Norway has one of the best mobile data networks in the world.

Before making the move, be sure to check that your current mobile phone is unlocked. This will allow you to easily swap out the SIM card to a new provider of your choice.

# Setting up a bank account

GETTING SETUP

You'll find the Norwegian financial system to be advanced, cheap, and fast overall. The country has long gone down the route of digitization, and cash is rarely used these days. So, once you're in the banking system everything just works.

However, getting into the Norwegian banking system as a foreigner is not so straightforward, especially for those coming from non-EU countries. Instead, you'll find getting started is rather old-fashioned and can be very slow. It typically takes anywhere from six to eight weeks to get fully set up, with lots of paperwork and several in-person trips to the bank. Once you've done that, it'll probably be the last time you have to visit a bank. Everything else is online or in an app.

The largest bank in Norway is DNB, and it's the one generally used by expats. There is also SpareBank 1 as another option.

If you need access to Norwegian banking faster, or need accounts in several countries, I recommend using Wise.com. It offers the best rates for currency conversion and allows you to open accounts in multiple denominations including Norwegian kroner (NOK).

# Getting your Vipps on

GETTING SETUP

As you start to explore Norway, you'll hear the Norwegians making a cute little sound asking about "Vipps?" They're not asking for a candy but instead talking about the payment app Vipps, from Norway's largest bank DNB. However, you don't have to be a DNB customer to use Vipps because it works with all banks. That makes it easy for friends to request and send money to each other regardless of their bank. Pretty much all Norwegians use Vipps, from little kids to sweet old grandmas selling wool sweaters.

Once you have your Norwegian bank accounts set up, download the app to get started. Note that you might have to set up a new app store account based in Norway. This includes adding a Norway-based credit card to your account.

The app itself is simple and straightforward. It works well in Norway because Norwegians don't like to owe others money. In fact, Norwegians don't like to have debt (even a small amount) to anyone or any business. This can make them uncomfortable, while at the same time it's also uncomfortable for them to ask for money. Enter Vipps, the easy way to both request or receive money. It'll even send you subtle reminders, so you never again forget you owe Jonas NOK150 for a beer last weekend.

# Dressing like a Norwegian

By European standards especially, but even by American standards, the Norwegian dress code would be considered informal and casual. In Norway it's less important to display one's wealth through fashion than you might see elsewhere. That's something only the Swedes really do here in Scandinavia.

You'll also notice Norwegians incorporate a lot of black and dark colors into their outfits, enough to make even a high school goth kid jealous. The typical Norwegian outfit may consist of black on black on black with a splash of gray. This is actually part of the overall Scandinavian fashion aesthetic. Many have tried to explain why, but it probably comes down to the fact that tall gorgeous blond people simply look fabulous in all black.

If you're coming from a warmer region (so about 90% of the planet), please allow me to introduce you to your new best friend . . . wool! This tried and true material is your key to surviving the cold Norwegian winter.

Finally, you may see Norwegians wearing athletic gear even when not exercising. That's because they are probably on their way to do just that or at least they want to give the impression they are.

# Understanding The Law of Jante

# (Janteloven)

GETTING SETUP

The Law of Jante is a social concept created by Danish-Norwegian author Aksel Sandemose in his 1933 book “A Fugitive Crosses His Tracks.” You may be familiar with a similar concept used in other parts of the world called “tall poppy syndrome.” In Janteloven, individual success is discouraged and, in many cases, considered inappropriate. Instead, society encourages the good of the collective over any one individual. This has shaped Scandinavian culture over many years and helped to create the peaceful, modest, and very homogenous society of today.

The Law of Jante

- You’re not to think you are anything special.
- You’re not to think you are as good as we are.
- You’re not to think you are smarter than we are.
- You’re not to imagine yourself better than we are.
- You’re not to think you know more than we do.
- You’re not to think you are more important than we are.
- You’re not to think you are good at anything.
- You’re not to laugh at us.
- You’re not to think anyone cares about you.
- You’re not to think you can teach us anything.

Failing to respect the Law of Jante can dramatically decrease your likelihood of success in business and hurt your relationships in Norway. However, as a foreigner you’ll be allowed to get away with some “exotic” behavior, such as giving a stranger a compliment.

# Getting healthcare

GETTING SETUP

For many foreigners (especially us Americans) it's fun to joke, "I'm in Norway, yay, free healthcare!" However, you'll soon find out that in Norway very little is free. You'll certainly be paying for the healthcare via your high taxes. And you still need to spend money from time to time to see a doctor or get a certain test. If you want to see a doctor fast, for example, at a private clinic, you will most certainly pay, and handsomely.

At the same time, the Norwegian healthcare system is good at doing its job of taking care of everyone, regardless of age or employment status. Even us non-Norwegians and non-citizen residents get things pretty good. If you have long-term or chronic health concerns, you'll be taken care of without any big medical bills to ever worry about.

Once you have established residency, you'll be able to access *Helse Norge* (Health Norway) and manage your healthcare from a single place. Here you can book appointments, find your doctor, get meds, and see test results.

# Learning the Norwegian language

GETTING SETUP

Thanks to a robust education system and lots of bad American television and movies, the majority of Norwegians speak perfectly good English! It's not hard to communicate both in public and business settings.

That being said, learning even a small amount of Norwegian can help you build camaraderie with Norwegians. If you plan to stay in Norway for a while, there is some expectation in society that you'll learn the language. Foreigners that stay here for five or more years can be looked down upon if they have yet to grasp the language, so it's recommended you make some effort in this area. It's typically always best to show both some admiration of and desire to learn the language to your work colleagues as well.

Your pronunciation will likely be dreadful at first, and if Norwegians see you struggle, they'll be eager to switch to English for your comfort and theirs. However, if you let them know you're really trying to learn and appreciate their support it'll go a long way. Although Norwegians are typically too polite to correct your bad Norwegian.

Want some help learning the language? Join a *Sprakkafe* to meet up and practice with other immigrants. Scan this QR code to learn more.

**Sprak Cafe**

**sprakkafe.no**

# HOW TO

# GET AROUND

12

One thing that I'm still impressed by to this day is how easy it is to move around Norway. And you might think this is not such an easy country to navigate, being so long and with ever-changing terrain. However, Norwegians are explorers, so it's perhaps not too surprising there are many, many ways to journey through the country.

Those landing in the capital city of Oslo will have no shortage of modes of transportation. From *trikken* (the tram), to *T-banen* (the subway), and *bussen* (the bus). On top of that, there are many players offering bikes, electric scooters, and whatever else can fit into an app. Oslo itself is a shining example of what all the hipsters call "urban mobility," which just means you're not going to spend half your day stuck in traffic.

For those in smaller Norwegian cities, don't worry, you won't be left walking. Any city of a decent size will also have several transportation options, although the smaller the city, the more likely it is you'll need a car.

And finally, for those brave souls trying to survive in rural Norway, first of all my condolences. Second, check with your local *kommune* (local county), because even in the middle of nowhere, the state tries to provide some options.

# Rules for sitting on public transportation

HOW TO GET AROUND

It should be noted that there are certain rules for sitting on public transportation in Norway. One does not simply sit next to a stranger in this country. If you see open seats or open benches, you must always take them. Don't just take the closest seat, which might already have someone sitting next to it. This will make Norwegians nervous, and they'll wonder why you're sitting so close. That's because Norwegians only get very close to strangers when they're incredibly drunk, not on the commute home from work at 3:30 p.m.

You also don't talk on public transportation, ever. You don't take loud phone calls, or even chat with a friend you're traveling with. You just sit there quietly and look out the window. Whatever you do, do not strike up a conversation with a stranger on public transportation or give them a compliment.

Finally, if you happen to be in the unfortunate situation of being on a bench and blocked from the aisle but needing to get off, don't ask the person to move or say "excuse me." You just kind of make a brief motion of getting up to signal them. That or you smash the stop button repeatedly so they can anticipate your move without having to speak to you.

# From the airport in style (and speed)

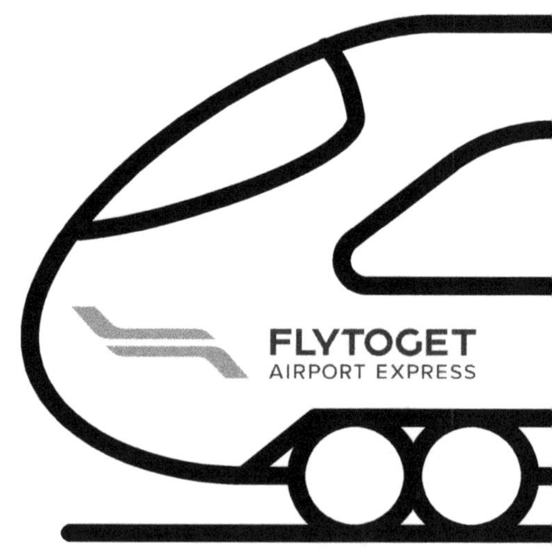


HOW TO GET AROUND

Living in Norway usually involves a fair amount of air travel. You often must get back to your home country or to travel within Norway itself. This isn't exactly an easy country to drive around with all the fjords and mountains.

So, when you're coming in and out of Oslo Airport, you'll want to take the Flytoget train. Look for the orange and gray signs and the slick futuristic train itself. It leaves every 20 minutes or so and gets you into downtown Oslo super quick. Download the official Flytoget app and you can get on and off even faster.

At smaller airports around Norway, there might not be an airport train but instead an airport bus is known as the *flybussen*.

# Getting a Norwegian driver's license

HOW TO GET AROUND

Depending on where you end up settling in Norway, you may need a car and, therefore, a Norwegian driver's license. If you call Oslo home, there's a good chance you can get by without a car and just use public transportation. Everywhere else, especially the smaller villages in Norway, you may need to be more mobile.

New arrivals in Norway can likely get by driving on their home country's driver's license for a short period of time. But please be advised there are certain time limits to when you must exchange your international driver's license for a Norwegian one. Failing to do so in time means you'll basically need to start from scratch with all the Norwegian driving training.

This requires several classes and passing a driving test. Additionally, there's a significant cost to satisfy all the requirements. Depending on your situation you can expect to pay NOK25,000–50,000 to complete everything. This is the same for those coming to Norway without a driver's license.

Driving in Norway is very easy and safe. There have been large investments in road infrastructure in Norway so there are many wide open freeways and tunnels to enjoy. Oh, and those Norwegians are far too shy to honk their horns or drive too aggressively.

# Buy a Tesla

HOW TO GET AROUND

If you really want to get around like a true Norwegian, you'll need to get yourself a Tesla. You'll notice almost immediately that Teslas are *everywhere* in Norway. Their arrival was a bit of a perfect storm, here's why.

The Tesla embodies many of the same attributes as the Norwegian. They're well designed, slick even. They're environmentally friendly. Finally, they allow you to signal you have some wealth, without being too braggy about it. All of the above could be said when describing Norwegian culture itself.

On top of that, in Norway Teslas were some of the most affordable cars you could buy. You were given huge tax breaks and a reduction of road tolls, which could save you thousands of *kroner* per year. Some of these sweet deals have expired now, but nevertheless, Norwegians caught the Tesla bug, and they dominate the road.

Not ready to buy your own Telsa? You can also rent them out short-term from a Norwegian company called Getaround (Formely Nabobil).

Scan the QR page on this page to get 200kr off your first ride.

**Getaround**

**bit.ly/NorwayRide**

# Rules for elevators in Norway

HOW TO GET AROUND

Many of the same rules that apply to public transportation in Norway also apply to using an elevator. The rules are perhaps even more important here because of the very confined space of the elevator.

Norwegians, you'll find, are slippery fish. In most social and even work situations, they always want an escape route, a way to get out of a conversation or awkward moment. Herein lies the problem when it comes to using an elevator. There's no escape.

So, help keep a Norwegian's stress level low by following these simple rules for elevators in Norway:

- If there are already three in an elevator, take the next one.
- While standing in the elevator, look straight at the door.
- Do not block the buttons or offer to push buttons for others.
- Do not say goodbye when others depart the elevator, just look at your shoes until the door closes again

# LIVE LIKE A NORWEGIAN

What does it mean to become Norwegian? You'll get different answers from different people. For many it's just a matter of being content with what you have. You have a good and secure job. The government takes good care of the people. The bus is always on time. Just appreciating these things could make one Norwegian to some extent.

To really become Norwegian though (I'm talking born with skis on your feet and oil running through your veins Norwegian) is not something most foreigners can achieve. Many would even say you don't really start to become Norwegian until you've lived here for ten years or more. Truthfully, it does take about that long to really belong in Norway.

There are, however, a few things you can do to become just a little more Norwegian. With the homogenous culture you find in Norway, becoming Norwegian is more about just becoming more like everyone else.

# Get your tax card

LIVE LIKE A NORWEGIAN

Perhaps one of the most Norwegian things you can do is pay your taxes. Norwegians are happy and even proud to pay the high taxes found in Norway. This might be because as you live in Norway, you realize you “get a lot for your money” when it comes to taxes paid and your quality of life. You’ll never have to worry about healthcare, and if you hit a rough spot, the Norwegian government will help you get back on your feet. This is regardless of whether you’re a citizen or not. All tax-paying residents, including expats, get the same access.

The starting point on your Norwegian tax journey is what’s called the “tax card,” although in such a digital society it’s not a physical card any more. You look it up and manage it online.

You can find your tax card at *Skatteetaten* (the Norwegian Tax Administration). Here you can update your most recent information, and it will automatically determine your tax rate. When you’re employed in Norway the company will “pull your tax card” to determine taxes to withhold on payday.

If you're new to Norway don't forget to check this before starting work. If an employer is unable to get your tax card you'll be taxed at the default rate of 50%.

# Go cross country skiing

LIVE LIKE A NORWEGIAN

For Norwegians, an activity such as cross-country skiing is one way relationships are strengthened. In addition to strengthening your muscles! We do a physical activity together, and that usually includes some element of suffering or hard work, and then after that we can begin to build trust together. Therefore, look out for invitations to ski from your new Norwegian friends. This might be your best (only?) chance to get to know them better.

It's important to let those of you who have never cross-country skied know that it can be very difficult. You'll likely fall many times your first time as you try to keep your balance about as well as Bambi on ice. However, if you get back up and keep trying you'll earn respect from your Norwegian friends. Even if you're a proficient alpine skier or snowboarder, don't get discouraged if it takes some time to learn how to cross-country well.

For Norwegians cross-country skiing is somewhat of national identity. As the old saying goes Norwegians are "born with skis on their feet". For confirmation one simply needs to look at the medal counts at the Winter Olympics to see how important the sport is to Norway. There's much excitement during the Olympics as it's one of the few times when the Norwegians can consistently beat the Swedes at something. It's recommended you cheer along with them during these times.

# Try brunost

LIVE LIKE A NORWEGIAN

As a newcomer to Norway many locals will ask you if you've had the *brunost*, aka the brown cheese, yet and what you think of it. So, it's best to quickly try it and get that out of the way.

I think many Norwegians enjoy offering *brunost* as a cruel trick, the classic "let's make the foreigner try our strange food" gag. However, many (myself included) find brunost to be quite tasty! It's high in sugar and it is like cheese, so for an American that's pretty much our two main food groups. It's technically not cheese, more of a by-product of cheese production itself. Most countries would throw it out, but during Norway's more humble and poorer times they added sugar to provide additional food for the people.

So *brunost* is considered an important part of cultural identity for Norwegians.

Give it a try, it's especially good on waffles.

# Attend a Nachspiel

LIVE LIKE A NORWEGIAN

The *nachspiel*, or the after party. Popular with Norwegian college kids but it's something that all Norwegians embrace and enjoy. Along with such a strong drinking culture in Norway there's also a saying that goes "getting half drunk is a waste of money". That's because alcohol is so expensive in Norway that once you start drinking you might as well go all the way, and then some. That's when the *nachspiel* comes into play, because at some point even the bars must close.

At this point of the night it's getting late, or early the following day, depending on how you look at it. It's far too late to buy alcohol anywhere, so you head back to someone's apartment to raid whatever is left there. Much to the neighbors' dismay these parties can get rowdy and go on late even until sunrise.

This is the point of the night where things are best described as getting "sloppy" or borderline absurd. Everyone has had far too much to drink, and it's all a bit last man or woman standing. If you're a foreigner that probably won't be you, as Norwegians have great stamina in the area of marathon drinking. If you're lucky enough to make an early exit, try to sneak out quietly. Otherwise, you risk having to take a "penalty shot" for your early departure, one final shot of aquavit for the road.

# Make Friday tacos

LIVE LIKE A NORWEGIAN

At some point in the 90s Norwegians were introduced to tacos, and the love affair has only grown and grown over the years. A major driving force of this is Taco Friday, or *tacofredag*. Every Friday across the country Norwegians get together to make tacos. It's estimated that each week, at least 13% of the country is doing just this.

Originally introduced to Norway by the USA, the tacos here take several forms. Often using a soft burrito instead of a hard corn shell, they can best be described as "TexMex," which is slightly different from traditional Mexican tacos. Along with that you can expect very little spice and, for some unknown reason, cold corn added to everything.

It's a well-beloved tradition in Norway and a great opportunity for social dinners. If you're lucky enough to get an invite to *tacofredag* from a Norwegian, be sure to accept it. This might be your best chance to get to know them.

# Get koselig and light a candle or two (or 20)

Some have said that work-life balance is difficult to achieve in the modern age. After all, we're always just an email or Facebook notification away when needed. Norwegians, on the other hand, have done well to ensure they take ample time to shut off work and enjoy life. This usually takes the form of trips to the cabin, enjoying nature or simply getting cozy (known as *koselig* in Norwegian) at home with a nice book and the candles lit.

Norwegians are sure to get plenty of *koselig* time in their life. As a foreigner in Norway, you're also entitled to the same time. Your Norwegian friends will expect you to have your personal cozy time and will think it's strange if you don't.

A key ingredient to *koselig* time involves candles. Lots of candles. If you're moving to Norway for love, be prepared for your partner to have candles everywhere. You'll be swimming in more wax than a Chapstick factory. It's that bad.

# Do a dugnad

LIVE LIKE A NORWEGIAN

A good opportunity to get to know more Norwegians, including your neighbors, is by joining a *dugnad*. This includes community work such as cutting trees, cleaning streets, or other volunteer activities. Often apartment buildings or neighborhoods will do a *dugnad* every year.

There is some expectation from society that you'll participate in these routines. No wonder everything is always so clean in Norway. It's also one of the few chances you might get to talk with a shy Norwegian.

Finally, Norwegians will also give you respect for doing a *dugnad*. It's a sign you want to contribute to society and don't mind putting in the work.

# Go to the hytte

LIVE LIKE A NORWEGIAN

Cabin life, or perhaps more appropriately cabin culture, is a big deal in Norway. It's not considered extravagant to have a holiday home in the form of a Norwegian cabin, the *hytte*. Many Norwegians do, or at the very least, have access to one through their family.

Oh, and in typical Nordic equality style, if you can't afford a holiday cabin, the government will even provide that for you. Yes, it's true. As a resident you can rent one from the government for very fair prices. The service is provided by the Norwegian Trekking Association, or *Den Norske Turistforening*.

In terms of what happens at the *hytte*, well it's really all about relaxing and enjoying nature. In fact, the further in the middle of nature your cabin is the more relaxing it is considered. Even if that means you must hike a significant distance to get to it. Norwegians like to boast about how far their cabins are in the woods or how 'off the grid' it is. Of course, with rise of wealth in Norway some cabins are also super modern with jacuzzies and WIFI.

When going to hytte be sure to find out if you need to bring anything. Often, you'll have to bring your own bedsheets and of course some games and snacks to enjoy by the fire.

# Pitch a tent anywhere thanks to allemannsrett

LIVE LIKE A NORWEGIAN

Norwegians are very proud of the rich nature found throughout their country, so much so that the government and the people felt it necessary to establish a law allowing for public access to it. It's called *allemannsretten*, or the freedom to roam.

Unlike in some countries where camping is limited to certain areas and requires a fee, in Norway, you can camp pretty much anywhere you like.

Norwegians also have great respect for their nature and generally take a 'leave it as you found it approach' to experiencing it. As a result, you won't find litter or other signs of humans as you explore off the beaten path. You also won't find many fences or safety signs even in areas that many would consider potentially unsafe! To put up such fences or signs even on popular tourist spots would take away from nature itself. Society instead follows a commonsense approach to exercising their rights to *allemannsretten*. They also follow 'the mountain weather rules' that you'll learn about later in this book.

However, perhaps it should be noted that it's not recommended to set up a tent on private property, say, your neighbor's front yard. While they are unlikely to call the cops, they will find you rather strange and probably avoid you.

# Try snus

LIVE LIKE A NORWEGIAN

If you spend any time in Norway, you'll notice locals putting small white packets in and out of their mouths. This is called *snus*, or tobacco packets. It's very popular, especially with younger Norwegians, and in many cases more popular than even smoking. It's also popular in Sweden where today most of the *snus* is produced.

It's a terrible and addictive habit and should be avoided at all costs. That being said, if you do enjoy tobacco, you'll probably enjoy *snus* as well. It's akin to smoking two or three cigarettes at the same time. You get a massive kick and don't even have to stand outside or get that smoke smell on you. It's also nearly impossible to stop, so proceed with caution.

But you will earn a few integration kudos from Norwegians if you give it a try. Make sure they don't encourage you to try the really strong *snus* after a night of drinking. You're certain to pass out in this case, or worse . . .

# Eat a Kvik Lunsj on top of a mountain

LIVE LIKE A NORWEGIAN

“Take a hike!” Literally.

Not everybody actually does it, but everybody likes to give the impression they do it, and everybody at the very least talks about it. Norwegians love exercise!

When you go on a hike in Norway, and be prepared, you will go on a lot of damn hikes, there’s a bit of a tradition. When you get to the top of the mountain you take a break. Everyone catches their breath, and you enjoy the view. Next someone brings out something very important to the hike. The *Kvikk Lunsj* candy bar, which my fellow Americans will recognize as being like a KitKat bar.

You could say this is the iconic Norwegian chocolate for every hike. It’s especially necessary around Easter time when many Norwegians have time off and the weather is just starting to turn warmer. During this time of the year, you’ll also for some unknown reason eat an orange along with your *Kvikk Lunsj* at the top of the mountain. Perhaps both help to give you a little jolt of energy to make it back to the bottom.

# Attend a julebord

The apex of Norwegian drinking culture and holiday celebration is the *julebord*, or Christmas party. A year's worth of pent-up frustrations is released on this glorious night. It's a bit of a fancy night, at least fancier than a typical Norwegian event, often taking place in a luxury hotel or other fine establishment. This is one night of the year when it's OK to indulge a little (more like a lot). You've almost made it through the brutal winter, so perhaps you've earned it after all.

And indulge the typical Norwegian does at *julebord*. The night is full of lots of great food, comfort food, songs, and dancing. However, much of the indulgence takes the form of consuming a large amount of alcohol. A table setting might include beer and wine, and of course, aquavit. As you can imagine, these events can go on well into the night.

Much has been said and debated about *julebord*, but most Norwegians seem to take the Las Vegas approach: what happens at *julebord* stays at *julebord*. In Norway, there are so many social codes that must not be broken, but on this wonderful night of the year, many of those rules fly out the window. You can be a little more wild than usual. You can say a few inappropriate things. You can sleep with a colleague, even if he or she is married! All that really matters is that you don't talk about it the next day. Or ever again.

# Watch 'Grevinnen og hovmesteren' on Christmas Eve

LIVE LIKE A NORWEGIAN

There's an unlikely popular show that airs in Norway every Christmas Eve or *julaften*, as it's called in Norway. The eighteen-minute comedy sketch is titled "Grevinnen og Hovmesteren" or "The Baroness and the Butler." Sometimes it's also called "Dinner for One."

It was originally recorded in Germany in 1963 for an English audience there. However, the sketch has become significantly more popular in Norway than it ever was in Germany. No one is really sure why, and most Norwegians don't even recall the actual name of the show! They do, however, always make time to watch it every year out of tradition.

The plot is humorous and basically involves a wealthy baroness getting the butler completely intoxicated. From there it's implied that part of his duties for the evening also include giving the old lady a good shagging.

What this has to do with the holidays I have no idea, although it certainly has a few things in common with the aggressive drinking culture in Norway, especially around the holidays.

# See the Northern Lights

LIVE LIKE A NORWEGIAN

Ah yes, the famed northern lights, aka aurora borealis, can certainly be found in Norway. You've seen the Instagram posts, and now it's time to see them for yourself in person. It's a truly unique Nordic experience and is highly recommended to check out.

If you find yourself in a southern part of the country, such as Oslo, you will unfortunately not be greeted with nightly shows from your balcony. To see the northern lights you need to go, surprise surprise, far up north. Although at certain times northern lights can be seen just a few hours' drive from Oslo, it's best to go all the way to the top, specifically the Tromsø or Alta regions.

The best time to see the northern lights is between the beginning of September and mid-April every year. It takes both a bit of planning and some good luck to see the lights. So be sure to give yourself a few days or longer to have a few attempts. Things such as overcast skies can limit your visibility, and much like many things in Norway, the weather can be unpredictable.

# See a fjord

LIVE LIKE A NORWEGIAN

*Fjord* in its basic meaning “where one fares through” has the same origin as the verb fare (travel) and the noun ferry. The narrow canyons with steep sides called *fjords* were formed by giant glaciers slowly moving across the land and carving these paths. They are quite breathtaking to experience and just one of the many unique types of nature you find in Norway.

To find most of Norway’s *fjords* you’ll have to head west. The majority of them can be found on the west coast around the areas of Bergen, Flåm, and Stavanger. Although technically even Oslo has its own fjord.

Perhaps arguably the most beautiful fjord in Norway is Geirangerfjord, which is also a UNESCO World Heritage site. Although when it comes to fjords, much like Norwegians themselves, they are all very nice to look at.

# Jump in a fjord, preferably a very cold one

Once you've made your way to your first *fjord* and taken your Instagram photos, there's one more thing you need to do. That is to jump in the damn thing! Bonus points if it's cold, and even more bonus points if it's freezing cold.

Norwegians take great pride in their beautiful nature. Furthermore, they take even more pride in showing it to foreigners and seeing them enjoy it as well. So don't be surprised if they randomly pull over the car to take a quick swim, or if they invite you to a (sometimes very cold) swim in the morning. These impromptu swims often occur in the many *fjords* found in Norway.

As a foreigner if jump in along with your fellow Norwegians you'll earn some respect. You might not be able to feel your fingertips but nevertheless respect will be earned.

# Buy a Douchebag

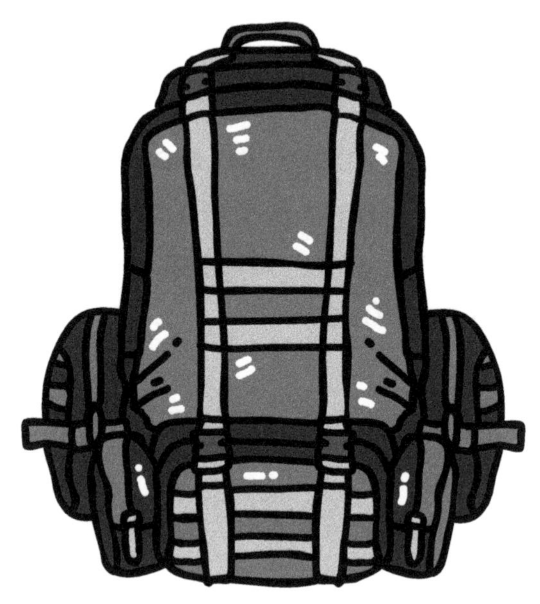

LIVE LIKE A NORWEGIAN

There's one easy way to spot a Norwegian in the airport. Look for the Douchebag!

Ok, that sounds perhaps worse than it really is. Because that's not to say that all Norwegians are douchebags. Truth be told, very few are. However, many, many Norwegians carry a Douchebag, which is a brand of travel luggage and backpacks with a funny name. More recently they have rebranded themselves to just Db, a less funny name, but it's still an amazing bag.

It won't be long until you spot a friend or colleague in Norway with a Douchebag. Once you're impressed and ready to join the Norwegian masses, swing by their website to pick up your own.

Scan the below QR code to get a 15% discount on your first order.

# Try Sheeps Head

LIVE LIKE A NORWEGIAN

When you're truly ready to prove your Norwegian-ness you're ready for one of the final bosses in the battle of integration. Enter, *smalahove*, or boiled sheep's head.

It's a brutal dish that hails back to more meager times in Western Norway. In towns such as Voss, Norway, the sheep's head was eaten to waste nothing when food supplies were low. Today it's still served to locals and brave tourists alike.

You'll likely find *smalahove* meat to be quite tasty and salty. Most people do, but it's the skull you might not enjoy so much as it slowly reveals itself with each bite. If you can stomach that (literally) then you're ready for the final *smalahove* challenge, to eat the eyeball in one gulp. Some people say it tastes like a runny egg. To others it's the ultimate sign of bravery in Norway.

Make sure you have some aquavit close by to wash it down.

# Become atheist

## (or at least act like one)

LIVE LIKE A NORWEGIAN

Norway is often described as one of the world's most secular countries. Only about 2% of Norwegians attend church regularly. I guess when your ancestors had ancient gods like Odin and Thor, it's tough to get excited about some new guy. On top of that, most Norwegians would rather spend their Sundays hiking, going to the *hytte*, or just getting *koselig*.

So, religion does not make for a big part of most Norwegians' lives. In fact, it's better not to bring the topic up at all. Especially at work. You will, however, notice there are many religious holidays in Norway. Most Norwegians won't know why exactly it's a holiday, but nevertheless they'll enjoy taking the extra time off. Norwegians who don't consider themselves very religious will also participate in religious ceremonies such as a confirmation or baptism. The country is dominated by Lutheran Christianity with 68% of the country belonging to the Evangelical Lutheran Church of Norway. That number is deceptive though, as newborns are automatically registered as part of the church. You actually need to go online to opt out of inclusion.

It should be noted that while Norway is not a very religious country, it is a very tolerant country for religion. Everyone has the freedom to practice any religion they choose. It's just more of a society that does so privately.

# Make fun of the Swedes

Hej!

LIVE LIKE A NORWEGIAN

Norway and Sweden have a fighting brother and sister relationship that goes back well into the 1800s. After a few unions and a world war or two, things are still tense but friendly between the two countries. As part of that friendly back and forth, you are allowed and even expected to make fun of Swedes while in Norway. In fact, as a foreigner you'll be able to get away with even more jokes than, say, your typical Norwegian. It might also earn you some extra respect from your Norwegian friends and colleagues.

In terms of jokes to be made, it can be challenging. Basically, the Swedes are always better at pop music than the Norwegians, and the Norwegians are always better at skiing than the Swedes. The Swedes, however, are well known for coming to Norway to work the jobs Norwegians don't want to work, for example, as a waiter and basically any job in hospitality. So an easy joke to play on any Swede is to treat them just like that, your waiter. Ask them to get you a glass of water or take your plate back to the kitchen. Works every time!

You can also scan Norwegian newspapers to find a story or two shaming the Swedes. If the Swedes do something wrong or dumb, the Norwegian press will certainly talk about it. That can also make for some good joke material at the office the next day.

LIVE LIKE A NORWEGIAN

If there's one day in Norway every year that is everyone's favorite, it is without a doubt May 17 (*syttende mai*) aka National Day (*Nasjonaldagen*). It's a day to celebrate the signing of the Constitution of Norway on May 17, 1814. This signing stopped Norway being ceded to Sweden, and instead it became an independent kingdom. As you can imagine, the Swedes are still a bit salty over that one, and the Norwegians couldn't be happier about that.

So there is much celebration every year on May 17. The day can start in fabulous fashion with champagne for breakfast. From there the Norwegians put on their *bunader*, traditional Norwegian outfits, and head to the town. There you'll find many happy (and slightly drunk) Norwegians enjoying the day. You'll also be treated to a children's parade (*barneparade*), a long line of cute kids wearing *bunader* and waving Norwegian flags proudly.

Be sure to get some ice cream that day as well, and after all that fun (and champagne) you'll probably be in bed by 6 p.m.

# Play a Kahoot!

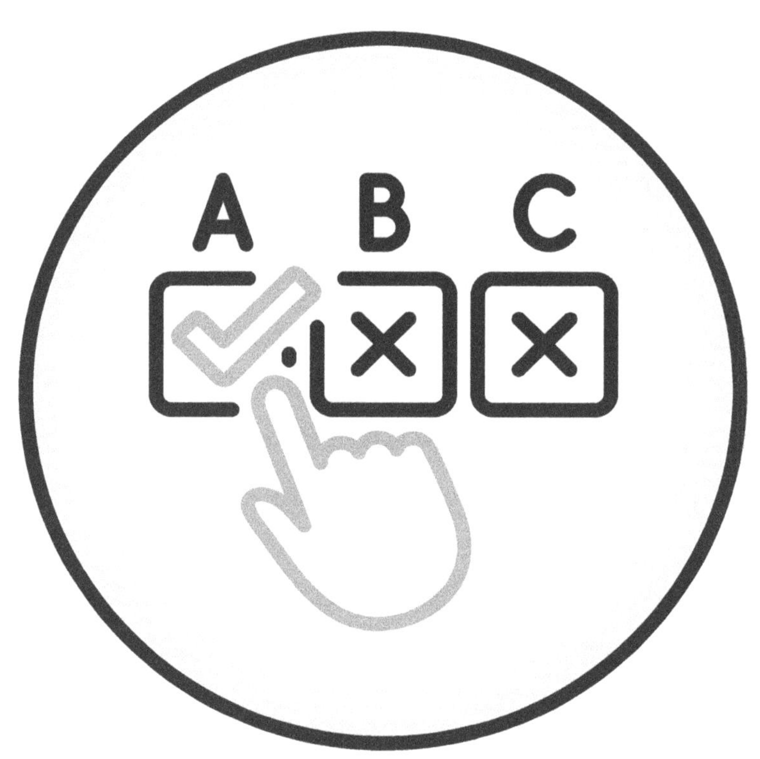

There is a bit of an unwritten rule in Norway that goes like this. If there are more than ten Norwegians in a meeting room, classroom, or auditorium . . . you must Kahoot!

What is Kahoot!?

Well, it's a fun quiz game you can play in a group with just your phones. Millions and millions of people Kahoot! every week at school or work. If you haven't heard about it, ask your kids.

While the game is played all around the world, it's extra popular in Norway as it was built and launched by Norwegians. So there's an extra pride in playing Kahoot! in Norway. On top of that, because of Norwegians' shy nature, they often use games or quizzes in social settings. It helps them get to know each other better and avoid their worst fear . . . having to make small talk.

# Become a Norwegian citizen

LIVE LIKE A NORWEGIAN

For my last and final suggestion on living like a Norwegian, I'll share perhaps the most Norwegian thing you can do, become a Norwegian citizen.

The good news is Norway does allow for you to become a citizen and even hold dual citizenship. So you don't have to completely give up on the motherland to enjoy the lifetime benefits of a Norwegian passport. There are also many benefits to having Norwegian citizenship in addition to the passport itself. First and foremost, you'll never have to navigate UDI again.

The best place to start when it comes to citizenship is the UDI website. Here you can look up your specific situation and what the current rules are. It also has detailed guides in several languages. In general, you need to have resided in Norway for at least seven years and have held valid resident permits during that time. Additionally, you need to pass an exam on Norwegian history and speak the Norwegian language to a certain level.

Having distant Norwegian relatives does not, unfortunately, get you a free pass to citizenship. But if you bring up this point Norwegians will think it's cute and smile.

# SURVIVAL GUIDE

Well you've made it this far, so before I close let's go through some of the longer-term survival needs of living with Norwegians. As you spend time in Norway, you'll notice people often ask you questions like, "How long have you been here?" and the sometimes more direct, "And do you plan to stay?" Norwegians ask these questions to a foreigner for a reason. They want to see if they have made it through the first few years. They know that many new arrivals to Norway don't.

That's because Norway can at times be a challenging place. It's not for everyone, and that's probably OK. From my experience, the biggest factors in failing to live with Norwegians come down to loneliness and, frankly, just being too damn cold. Now imagine those who are both cold and lonely. It's easy to see why coming to Norway for love is one of the main reasons people make the move. At least in that case you'll have someone to keep you warm!

So let's go through a few ways to hopefully help keep you social and even warm.

# Making friends in a shy country

SURVIVAL GUIDE

You'll face many challenges surviving Norway. One of the biggest challenges is going to be the loneness. It's a great country, but it's also a very cold country much of the year, and the Norwegians themselves can also be rather cold. It's not the Norwegians' fault: I don't think they realize how they are sometimes as cold as the weather. They probably don't know how much they at times challenge a foreigner's patience. And we foreigners often take our time to truly understand and respect this culture, or any new culture. As a result, there's a lot of misalignment of experiences and expectations between both parties. That makes for much stepping on toes in the great dance that is living with Norwegians.

So, you're cold, you're having trouble making new friends, and you're probably missing some random food ingredient from back home. What can you do about it?

A few quick tips:

- Join your fellow expats in the Facebook groups mentioned earlier in the book. You'll quickly meet some new friends who are ready to meet up and likely just as miserable as you are. Misery loves company!

- Invite new friends to dinner. Many shy Norwegians don't do this, so don't be offended if they don't offer. However, as a foreigner, it's ok to do so.

- Join social clubs around your hobbies or use social clubs to learn new hobbies. When Norwegians do things as a group, they are much more open to getting to know someone better. There are hundreds and more likely thousands of small social groups in Norway around just about any topic or interest.

- Do sports, not just for the exercise but to get to know someone better. While there is little talking during the actual sporting, afterward there's a chance to have a meal and better connect.

The hard truth about making friends with Norwegians is that it takes time. Like years. From talking with many other fellow expats, it seems after about 5 years most have 1 or 2 Norwegians whom they consider good friends. After 10 years you have a few more. This is different from other cultures where you might be able to make more close friends very quickly. However, some good news. While Norwegians are difficult to get close to once you're in you're usually in for life. If the trust is maintained between both parties you have likely made a loyal friend for life.

# Get care packages from home

SURVIVAL GUIDE

Missing something special from back home? Foreigners will find they miss the smallest things when they can't easily find them in Norway. Typically, these are food items, or as we call them back in the USA, comfort foods. But they can even be something as small as a certain ingredient or just a specific brand you like. In these cases, the best way to get these items to Norway is through a care package from home.

Unfortunately, you'll find that it's expensive to ship items from pretty much anywhere in the world to Norway. We basically live up in Santa's neighborhood, and at least he has those reindeer to get around. For the rest of us everything takes a *long* time to get shipped up to Norway. You'll help your friends or family members by encouraging them not to mail large or heavy boxes your way. It's best to optimize for the lightweight things you miss.

Furthermore, it's important to know about how customs (toll) work in Norway. Let me sum it up for you: it's a complete pain in the ass and expensive. This country loves to tax things so much, they even tax candy from Grandma coming into the country. Tell friends and family members sending you care packages to write multiple names on the package to split the tax liability between more people. On the customs declaration they should say the items have low value or write "GIFT" in big black marker.

# Sleeping with Norwegians

SURVIVAL GUIDE

Norway's greatest importer of foreigners is not immigration or job placements but love itself. And there's no shortage of ridiculously good-looking people to fall in love with here, even if it's just for one night. If you're reading this book, there's a high chance you already have. For those without a Norwegian to call their own, this can make it tough to survive the loneliness of Norway. Especially during the wintertime.

If you are, however, lucky enough to sleep with a Norwegian, or two, or twelve during your adventures, there are a few social norms to understand. The first is that casual sex is fairly prevalent both in Norway and throughout the Nordic countries. So slow down there, tiger, and try to avoid falling too head over heels in love after just a single hot night under the sheets. There's a high likelihood that the experience, as passionate as it might have been, is taken less seriously by your Norwegian partner.

When it comes to sex and relationships Norwegians also seem to do things backward, at least compared to my own culture. They normally sleep with you a few times *before* they decide if they want to date you. In America, you would usually go on a few dates first and *maybe* get lucky.

# Shopping in Sweden

SURVIVAL GUIDE

It’s not too long before you realize that living in Norway is expensive, especially when it comes to food. When it comes to the grocery store, you may also find it has less selection than your home country and at about double the price, or more. So, one must be sneaky to survive in Norway, at least to feed oneself.

We do this by making a trip down to Sweden, where the selection is larger and the taxes much lower. This is also basically the only tax avoidance that’s allowed by Norwegian society. And it is delicious. Of course, there are some quotas on what you’re allowed to bring back into Norway. This is especially true around the most popular products of alcohol and tobacco products.

Once this became a thing (and was even given a nickname of ‘*harryhandel*’) an unsurprising thing happened. The Swedes, ever the exporters of things, set up huge malls right at the Norwegian border. Now countless Norwegians cross the border to pick up their bacon, cheese, snus, and candy in bulk.

This survival trip is most relevant to those who live in Southern Norway with close access to the border. For everyone else, you’ll have to get your deals at the airport in the duty-free stores.

SURVIVAL GUIDE

My next Norway survival tip is for the truly desperate, those who have given up on hope or are just very, very broke. Being broke in Norway means you certainly can't afford to go to a restaurant, even a bad one. You probably also can't afford to get a bag of groceries. If this sounds at all familiar then you are probably a college student. In that case you might already know about the almighty Grandiosa pizza.

It's the cheapest large frozen pizza you can get in Norway. It fills you up good, but at what cost?

The ingredients include some type of cardboard and what appears to have been a cheese-like product. It's awful, and Norwegians can't stop buying it. Grandiosa sells more than 25 million pizzas a year in a country that only has 5 million residents.

Still, when you're desperate you're desperate. Try to eat them only after 2 a.m. if possible.

# Go out in the sun, even if it's winter

SURVIVAL GUIDE

I'm fairly convinced the main reason some foreigners don't last the first year of life in Norway is simply vitamin D deficiency. Yes, all the jokes about bad weather in Norway are probably true. We simply don't get much sun here on top of the globe. That reminds me of one of my favorite quotes from Norway: "I love the Norwegian summer, it's the best day of year!"

Truth be told, a Norwegian summer is pretty nice. Sure, it doesn't last as long as it does in other parts of the world, but nevertheless, there are many glorious and warm days all throughout July, at least in the lower half of Norway.

However, you'll notice a funny thing happens when the sun does come out, even if the weather is still very cold outside. The Norwegians emerge and follow the sun much like a flower in bloom. They'll sit outside cafes or on their patios in winter coats with only their faces exposed. They do this to soak up any ray of sunshine they can get, storing the precious sun energy much like a squirrel store nuts.

You should learn to do the same. Even an extra five minutes of sun on your face can make all the difference.

# Take your Vitamin D

SURVIVAL GUIDE

For the cold and long months when you can't get enough sun, you'll need to supplement your body. Norwegians do this with vitamin D pills. You can find them in just about any supermarket (*matbutikk*) in dissolvable tablet form, or go to a pharmacy (*apotek*) for the actual pills. As I covered at the start of this book, you may find the Norwegian versions of vitamins usually have fairly low dosage. So you need to purchase the good stuff in your home country or online at iHerb for delivery to Norway.

It's also easily possible in Norway to get your vitamin D levels checked. This is something I, hailing from sunny California, had never had to do, but apparently it's very common in the Nordic countries. I guess for a Scandinavian it's the same as checking the oil in your car. It's good to do it at least once a year and top things up when needed.

It should also be noted that Norwegians, in addition to recommending you top up your vitamin D, will also try to get you to take *Tran*. Basically, it's fish oil. It's full of omega-3s and vitamin D as well.

If you can manage to drink this concoction, you're not just surviving Norway, you're pretty much already a Norwegian!

**iHerb Vitamin D**

**bit.ly/NorwayD**

# Go to Syden!

SURVIVAL GUIDE

At the risk of taking a third section of this book just to tell you get more sun, I have one more sun-related survival tip. And this is perhaps the best survival tip of them all. That's because when it comes to surviving life in Norway, sometimes the best thing you can do is get the hell out of the country.

This is what millions of Norwegians do each year, several times a year, but especially in the summer month of July. That is to go *syden*, which basically means to go south. Typically, this involves a trip to Spain, a favorite vacation spot for Norwegians, but it can also include places such as Greece. Even getting down the to southern Sweden is considered going *syden*. Just anywhere south, and by default, anywhere south can only be warmer and have more sun than Norway.

It's strange to me that in July, the only super sunny month in Norway, most Norwegians leave the country. Although as you've hopefully learned by now, when it comes to getting sun you need to maximize every opportunity. Norwegians will always understand this, and having a nice tan from your trip to *syden* is one way Norwegians show off to their friends. It's a subtle way to brag that you traveled and have the sun-kissed glow to prove it.

# Know the mountain weather rules

(FJELLVETTREGLENE)

SURVIVAL GUIDE

My last survival tip can save your life, and that's not the start of another bad joke. There is actually a set of rules that all Norwegians know called *fjellvettreglene*, or the mountain weather rules. While the nature of Norway is no doubt beautiful, it can also be dangerous for us non-Vikings if we don't know what we're doing. We're not just talking about going out on a small hiking trail in a government park. We're talking the real deal and, quite literally, out-in-the-middle-of-nowhere nature.

So since the 1930s the Norwegian government has shared some rules for the mountain. They have gone through a few iterations, with the last updated version of the rules being published in 2016. Get to know them know and be prepared for the inevitable mountain climb you'll be invited to in Norway.

**Tourist Assoc**

**bit.ly/NorwayUT**

# The Mountain Weather Rules

1. Plan your trip and report where you are going.

2. Adapt the trip according to ability and conditions.

3. Pay attention to weather and avalanche warnings.

4. Be prepared for storms and cold, even on short trips.

5. Bring the necessary equipment to be able to help yourself and others.

## The Mountain Weather Rules

6. Make safe choices. Recognize avalanche-prone terrain and unsafe ice.

7. Use a map and compass. Always know where you are.

8. Turn in time - there is no shame in turning around.

9. Save energy and seek shelter if necessary.

# CLOSING

So there you have it, many ideas for things to do to make living with Norwegians a little easier. Although if you managed to do even half the things mentioned in this book, I'm sure you would do just fine in Norway.

Truth be told, Norway is a lot like many other places. It is what you make of it. And as places where one can make it go, you certainly could do worse. All the peculiar things that come with living with Norwegians are perhaps not so important when one has such a nice place to live as Norway.

For the other foreigners out there in Norway, I get it. This is a country that is easy to fall in love with. Those Norwegians aren't exactly bad looking either. Just know that it's also a country that's often hard to tell if it loves you back. You'll need to earn that love, and it will take time. And lots of work. This struggle before the reward is the Norwegian way.

Norwegians themselves will want to change you or will want you to be more like them. I encourage you not to allow them to be entirely successful. While you'll need adapt yourself while living with Norwegians, they could also benefit from your own culture I'm sure.

# GLOSSARY

**BankID:** A way to validate your identity on Norwegian government and banking websites.

**Brunost:** A brown cheese (although typically a by-product of cheese production) considered an important part of cultural identity for Norwegians.

**D number:** A temporary resident number given to new arrivals. It's like a personal number used by a Norwegian citizen.

**Dugnad:** A social and volunteer culture activity where neighbors or colleagues get together to improve something together.

**DUF number:** A way to track your application through UDI for work and resident permits.

**Fjord:** Its basic meaning, "where one fares through," has the same origin as the verb fare (travel) and the noun ferry. The narrow canyons with steep sides called fjords were formed by giant glaciers slowly moving across the land and carving these paths.

**Kvikk Lunsj:** The Norwegian version of a KitKat bar. You eat these with your Norwegian colleagues after a good cross-country ski. Norwegians just love milk chocolate!

**Hytte:** A Norwegian cabin and where Norwegians go to relax and get away from things.

**Janteloven:** A social concept where individual success is discouraged and, in many cases, considered inappropriate.

**Julebord:** Literally meaning the Christmas table, it's a holiday dinner with friends or colleagues where everyone eats and drinks way too much.

**Kahoot!:** A Norwegian quiz game with catchy music that is often played at school and social events.

**Koselig:** Being cozy is something Norwegians enjoying doing and make ample time for. Often this is something as simple as lighting candles and reading a book.

**Nachspiel:** The Norwegian after party that can go very, very late into the evening or next day.

**Syden:** Meaning "to go south," it's something Norwegians do often to travel and get more sun.

**Vipps:** A peer-to-peer payment app used by almost all Norwegians that makes it easy to split bills and pay friends without the awkwardness of having to ask for money.

The valley my
Norwegian family came
from in Ølve, Norway

Our family name Storedale means 'big valley' in Norwegian. I'm told the name came to be because at the time this was considered a really big valley to them!

*This book is dedicated to my great Grandfather Baard Storedale. A Norwegian who immigrated to America in 1903. Through a strange series of events, our lives seemed to have reflected each other much like a mirror.*

*I hope that he found living with Americans as pleasant as I've found living with Norwegians.*

# DEDICATION

*Thanks to the many Norwegians who have shaped my experience in Norway. A few special thanks to the following:*

*Nanny: My love and the Norwegian I've had the great pleasure to live with. Even during lockdowns, you've made our place a sanctuary. Now please stop lighting so many damn candles.*

*Natalie: My upstairs neighbor whom I consider to be half American. Also, my first neighbor who didn't just tolerate karaoke, she encouraged it!*

*My Norwegian In-laws: My new family and the Norwegians who always have the best julebord.*

*Kristel: My forever friend and always a supporter of crazy ideas like this book. Also one of the brave people to attempt living with Norwegians.*

*Helle & Joakim: For all the god stemming and good times we have shared over the years. #floorgang*

*Stina & Kenneth: My favorite Norwegian pensioners living their best life in Spain and showing me the joys of syden life.*

# Need more help Living with Norwegians?

**Scan to buy**

Get the companion book to this one,
***Working with Norwegians***

Available on Amazon and direct at
**www.workingwithnorwegians.com**

ISBN: 9798629630937

Thanks for reading the book. In the spirit of the book and "pay it forward" culture, I encourage you to give the book to someone else who is new to Norway. Before you do that, sign your name below.

| Name \ Where are you from? | Date |
|---|---|
| ______________________________ | __________ |
| ______________________________ | __________ |
| ______________________________ | __________ |
| ______________________________ | __________ |
| ______________________________ | __________ |
| ______________________________ | __________ |
| ______________________________ | __________ |

**New to Norway Pro Tip:**

Use Bookis.com to resell this book and even get a chance to meet up with other book-loving Norwegians. Scan the QR code to get started.

**Bookis Marketplace**

**bookis.com**

www.ingramcontent.com/pod-product-compliance
Ingram Content Group UK Ltd.
Pitfield, Milton Keynes, MK11 3LW, UK
UKHW022021190726
13853UKWH00005B/2049